For
Uncle Raja,

A genuine rasikar & a critic whose views I value.

With Love,
Rajini

LONDON
9th October 2004

HYMNS AND SONGS

OF PURANDARADASA

Translated by

Dinesh Hassan

Harmony Series
Bottom Dog Press
Huron, Ohio

©copyright 2004
Dinesh Hassan & Bottom Dog Press
ISBN 0-933087-89-6

Bottom Dog Press
PO Box 425
Huron, Ohio 44839
http://members.aol.com/Lsmithdog/bottomdog

Acknowledgments

Cover Images:
Ramanathaswamy 12th Century Hindu Temple
© Philip Baird/ www.anthroarcheart.org
Cover Design: Jason Teply
Book Design: Larry Smith

For
Shiromani and her children

Contents

Introduction — 7
We Poor Milkmaids Are on Our Way to Sell Milk — 11
Why Have You Decreed this Fate for Me? — 13
This Life Is Hell, Yet I Am not Ready to Leave It — 14
Lord Hari, Why Have You Sent Me on a Visit to this Netherworld? —15
How Easy It is to Fake One's Devotion to Krishna! — 16
Why Do You Foolishly Punish Your Body? — 17
Drown Me or Keep Me Afloat — 18
Why Am I Not Worthy of Your Mercy, My Lord? — 19
Although You Are Mindful of My Woes — 20
I Have Not the Nerve to Come to You — 21
Muddle-Headed I Am — 22
Heralds of Death Have No Mercy — 23
Not Even You Can Override My Karma — 25
Children at Play Built a Nice Little House — 26
Accept this Hard Candy — 27
Plant the Seed Called Narayana — 28
Children Tease Me at Play, Mommy — 29
Take My Word for it, Hari Has No Time for this Music — 31
Trust, My Mind, Sri Krishna's Holy Feet — 32
Allow Me to Be Your Serf — 33
I Want to Know if My Lord Ranga Is About — 34
Goddess of Plenty — 35
May Calumniators Prosper — 36
Why Do People Say I Am Poor and Homeless? — 37
Who Among these Three Will Come to Your Aid? — 38
This Is No Time for Good People — 39
The World Is Too Much with Us — 40
Grant Me Lord Ranga — 41
Human Life Is Precious — 42
To Be Human Is to Let Hari's Name Forever Be on One's Tongue — 43
Have You Seen this Holy Child? — 44
O My Lord of the Wagging Tail — 45
Enough of this Hanging by People's Doorsteps, Krishna — 46
This Life Is a Debt Owed in Previous Incarnations — 47

We Love All, the Stingy and the Generous — 48
These Clowns Crack Me Up — 49
Trust Not this Shell, the Body — 50
What Greater Happiness Can There Be? — 51
If I Am Meditating on You — 52
Why Do I Need You, if I Am Girded by Your Holy Name?— 53
Lord Madhava, Let My Eyes Always Feast on
Your Divine Form — 54
O Yadava, Let Us See You — 55
My Sister, Grab that Earthen Pot — 56
Say Krishna Once in a While! — 57
Yashoda Keeps Her Divine Child Occupied — 58
Never Reached Home — 59
Please Don't Summon the Bogeyman, Mother — 60
Who Is at the Door? — 61
A Letter Has Arrived — 62
Sing Our Hari's Praise — 63
O Wandering Maiden, Won't You Summon Our
Handsome Lord? — 64
Who Is at the Door? — 65
Come What May, I Care Not — 66
My Home Is over There — 67
What Avails One, When Karma — 68
Try this Hubble-Bubble — 69
Have You Ever Seen Wasps Attack Live Coals? — 70
Offer Our Lord a Flower, He'll Feed Your Livestock
with Grass — 71
This Is My Trade — 72
Boatman, You Are My Hope — 73
Say Rama, Rama, Rama, Rama, Rama — 74
Spurn this Dog, Brothers — 75
Why Pretend with the Rest You Are Merciful? — 76
Why Do You Fret, My Poor Soul? — 77
Let the Crows Caw, Hari — 78
I Have Gone Plum Crazy — 79
I Will Not Stop Dogging You — 80
O Mother of Krishna — 81
[Notes — 82-85; Biographical Note on Author — 87]

Introduction

Devotional literature of India in its various languages records works in many genres and forms. One of the best known of them is the *Bhagavad Gita*, often translated into English under the name *The Song of God*. Also well known are the great Sanskrit epics, the *Ramayana* and the *Mahabharatha*. In recent years, Western readers have been well taught and nourished by the hymns and songs of devotion by the eighth century Indian Sufi saint Jalaluddin Rumi and the thirteenth century North Indian writer Kabir. Their work comes under the rubric *Bhakthi* (the way of devotion) in India.

Bhakthi is traditionally defined as a philosophy which promotes the view that God, Krishna in his many incarnations, is accessible to the devotee primarily through love. Ancient Hindu treatises hold that the sole means of reaching God is by performing Vedic (liturgical) rituals and reciting holy formulas, both of which were accessible only to the elite priestly class. Seeking to free the Hindu mind from its allegiance to the tyranny of Vedic texts, writers in the *bhakthi* tradition, calling themselves *dasa*s, servants, of Krishna, set out to domesticate Hindu truths in richly allusive and metaphorical language. Like the early Romantics in Western literature, they committed themselves to the idiom of their contemporaries, rather than mimicking a language from removed and mysterious times.

In compositions replete with references to Krishna's exploits in the scriptural and folk narratives about him, they create a mix of the learned and the proletarian styles, simultaneously using scriptural materials, proverbs, and folklore. They employ the imagery of everyday life to express some of the loftiest tenets of their faith as well as their personal observations.

The *bhakthi* movement flourished in the Southern Indian state of Karnataka between the 14th and 18th centuries. Purandaradasa, some of whose songs and hymns are Englished here, is the defining poet of this tradition. Scholars estimate that he was born in 1485 and died in 1565. Readers of this volume will certainly find it interesting that Purandaradasa is not just contemporaneous with John Donne and Shakespeare but also that in his works are present many of the Elizabethans' favorite techniques, especially the metaphysical conceit. Note the clarity and sharpness of the metaphor of the man who is forever begging others because he is without God's grace:

> The ungodly have money.
> I, their mindless serf,
> Tell them they have no equals.
> They give me a handful of sage.
> I suffer like a mouse that has eaten poisoned bait.

Look at the seriousness, conciseness, and the appropriateness of homely metaphors used to emphasize the transience of life:

> To the market came
> Many from different villages;
> When dusk fell,
> They left in many directions.

> A sparrow flew into the courtyard;
> And was gone within a minute.
> The lodger arrived at the inn,
> And left before sunrise.

    Such similarities are noteworthy if only because they show that regardless of their origins and philosophical doctrine, all religious writers mine the same resources of language.
    While other *bhakthi* poets seem to revel in the confidence that their devotion has made them one with their deity, much of Purandaradasa's work insistently speaks to the anxiety about the unavailability of God's mercy, a feature also found in John Donne and Gerard Manly Hopkins. In many of Purandaradasa's hymns, the anguished speaker cries out, demanding his Lord be worthy of being called the merciful one. He wants to know why myths about Him say that He has come to the aid of those who seek His assistance. Why then does He turn a deaf ear to this devotee's prayer?

The singer often reaches the paradoxical conclusion that God's name alone is enough to see him through his crises.

Like other religious writers, Purandaradasa has salvation much on his mind. But this preoccupation is sometimes expressed in a delightfully, deceitfully artful way. In a very popular satirical composition about the soul lost in its worldy obsessions, he compares it to a wandering dog, "O my Lord of the Wagging Tail." The dog is given to seeking what it cannot get, or seeking it in the wrong place, and receiving nothing but pain in return:

> Was your lordship led to the kitchen
> By the sweet smell of rice pudding?
> Did your lordship enjoy singing
> When your tail received a thwacking from the ladle?
>
> Were the odorific alleys to your lordship's liking?
> Please tell your servant
> What joy it was to roll in dust and ashes behind the kitchen.

Unlike most Western devotional poets, Purandaradasa covers a wide range of emotions in his works. The personas in his poems express tender love for Krishna in their roles as mothers and lovers. Listen, for instance, to the halfhearted entreaty made to Krishna's mother by lovelorn but fearful milkmaids smitten by him:

> How can we pay this stealer of his kisses his tax?
> Decked out in gold,
> Diamonds, emeralds, sapphires, rubies,
> He wants no money,
> But a kiss and a girdle-loosening hug.
> Make him listen to our entreaties,
> O mother of that blue-skinned rascal.

I do not claim his forward thinking and literary skills always raise Purandaradasa above his contemporaries or followers. Many of his compositions offer the Ten Commands variety advice on how to lead a good life. Some of them are included here. Sexual desire outside marriage is a frequently mentioned danger; so is the love of gold and land. Purandara Dasa, however different he is from his contemporaries, takes the old patriarchal stance about women. Some of his most popular songs, frequently performed by renowned musicians, contain platitudes of the dullest kind. Consider that every artist produces weaker work. At his strongest, this poet brings endless surprise and devastating entertainment.

Until about 1875, the Purandaradasa's work survived only in the oral tradition. It is hard to say just how many hymns and songs bearing the signature "Purandaravitthala" are by Purandaradasa himself. Many less talented composers certainly sought immortality for their inferior compositions by using the signature. Some nine hundred hymns bearing Purandaradasa's signature have appeared in various collections. The compositions here are representative. I have deliberately avoided translating those hymns which do not display Purandaradasa's trade mark, metaphysical wit.

I thank Larry Smith and Vanamala for their encouragement. I cannot thank Deborah Stokes enough for helping make the translations idiomatic. David Shevin is the guiding spirit behind the translations, but I alone am responsible for the clumsiness in the renderings.

Dinesh Hassan
Central State University
February 2004

Halu Maralu Bandevamma

(We Poor Milkmaids Are on Our Way to Sell Milk)

We poor milkmaids are on our way
To sell milk in town.
O mother of that purple-skinned rascal.

You know well how long it takes
For us to get ready to go to the market.
We are up before sunrise.
We don our best saris and wear
Our precious gold bangles.
Then we dance our way to town
With milk jugs on our jasmine-adorned heads.
No easy trick, mind you.

A few minutes into the trek,
Who do we see but your naughty little boy?
He wraps an arm around our waists,
Grabs a hand;
Says he will unwrap our saris
If we don't pay his tax.

How can we pay this stealer of kisses his tax?
Decked out in gold,
Diamonds, emeralds, sapphires, rubies,
He wants no money,
But a kiss and a girdle-loosening hug.
Make him listen to our entreaties,
O mother of that blue-skinned rascal.

You don't want us to be beaten black and blue
By our jealous husbands.
We wish we knew how to avoid him.

"Come here, pretty girl, I want to tell you a rumor,"
Says he.

Teach us how to resist the invitation.
The moment we near him,
His hands explore our hills and valleys.
Teach us how to break away from him.
Tell him to leave us alone.

No one will buy milk at noon.
And there is none left unspoiled
After we pay the tax demanded
By that blue-skinned little thief.
Please tell that little rascal,
Purandaravitthala, to leave us alone.

We poor milkmaids are on our way
To sell milk in town.

Ena Baredeyo?

(Why Have You Decreed this Fate for Me?)

Why have you decreed this fate for me,
O Brahma?
Why are you so unkind?
Why must I be bereft of pride?
Begging everybody for mere sustenance?

To prolong the agony of this six-inch stomach,
I stand by the door of the rich,
Bathing them in flattery,
Saying they are the paragons of virtue and looks.
They say,
"I promise, come again tomorrow.
I'll give you something."
I circle their homes
Like a mule tied on a long rope to a pole.

The ungodly have money.
I, their mindless serf,
Tell them they have no equals.
They give me a handful of sage.
I suffer like a mouse that has eaten poisoned bait.

I don't mind that you ordained this fate for me,
But please, please,
Spare my children and their children from a like fate.
I implore you, I beg you,
In the name of
Lord Purandaravitthala, Krishna of Udupi.

Why have you decreed this fate for me,
O Brahma?
Why are you so unkind?
Why must I be bereft of pride,
Begging everybody for my mere sustenance?

Illiralare, Allige Hogalare

(This Life Is Hell, Yet I Am not Ready to Leave It)

This life is hell,
Yet I cannot leave it.
O Lotus-Naveled One,
Guide me to your abode.

Don't care to live,
Don't care to die;
Don't care to suffer life's many slings and arrows,
Don't care to run from them.
O, Creator, humble cowherd,
Teach me ways to meditate on your holy feet.

I am too much in love
With bobbing in this boiling cauldron, life,
Too addicted to the pleasure of daily pain of life.
Guardian of cattle, son of Nanda,
Keep me in your thoughts forever.

Engulfed in the pleasurable darkness
Of wife, children, and friends,
I am unable catch a ray of your divine light.
Protector of supplicants,
Lord Udupi Krishna,
Purandaravitthala, have mercy on me.
Have mercy on me.

This life is hell,
Yet I am not ready to leave it.
O Lotus-Naveled One,
Guide me to your abode.

Yakennanni Rajyakelethande Hariye?

(Lord Hari, Why Have You Sent Me on a Visit to this Netherworld?)

Lord Hari,
Why have you sent me on a visit to this netherworld,
When you knew
You had no time
To guide me on my journey?

I don't know the lie of the land,
Nor are my limbs strong enough
To bear the burden of the travail.
A stranger am I to the creeds and dogmas of the natives.
No one is here to shelter, feed, or clothe me.
Only you know the ways of this world,
But won't tell me.

I have no kin here,
No well-wishers.
No patron, nothing heartening.
No coin, no stones, no hosts.
No inkling of what you know
Of this desolate, sinful patch of earth.

Not one person offers me food;
Not one person shows me kindness.
Lord of all,
There's no one to guide me to you.
My heart is weak, my faith wobbles.
Purandaravitthala, King of Kings,
You know all,
But won't tell.

Lord Hari, why in the name of Heaven,
Have you sent me on a visit to this netherworld,
When you knew you had no time to guide me on my journey?

Dasananthaguvenu Dhareyolage Nanu

(How Easy It Is to Fake One's Devotion to Krishna!)

How easy it is to fake one's devotion to Krishna!
You need not the slightest bit of sincerity
When you pretend to be a dasa.
I am no dasa.

My forehead is adorned with the vertical nama;
In my hand is carried the tell-tale brass pot.
I stride the streets in a loincloth.
Don't be fooled by my ascetic appearance, friends.
I am no dasa.

Earthly riches are my prime concern;
I have had no time to acquire spiritual wealth.
Counting my few pennies over and over,
I have never tried to cleanse my soul, friends.
I am no dasa.

Never had time to meditate on Lady Lakshmi's spouse;
Matins, masses, evensongs were no part of my clock.
I have nothing,
For I had no time to lovingly meditate
On the twin feet of my Lord Purandaravitthala.
I am no dasa.

How easy it is to fake one's devotion to Krishna!
You need not the slightest bit of sincerity
When you pretend to be a dasa.
I am no dasa.

Yake I Dehavanu Dandisuve Vyartha?

(Why Do You Foolishly Punish Your Body?)

Why do you foolishly torture your body,
When you might win merit
By single-mindedly contemplating
The name of Lakshmi's spouse?

What profits it you to scrub your body,
Sitting cross-legged, feasting on lusts,
Like a heron thinking on fish,
If you do not focus your mind
On the exploits of the slayer of demons?

Pretending to be meditating,
You are mentally multiplying your paltry pennies;
What profits you to sit cross-legged in that corner,
Unless you recite, recite,
And recite the myriad names of the Infinite One?
How else can you find fulfillment in life?

Remember, fool, Ajamila gained salvation
By calling on Narayana just once.
Doubt not, stop foolishly torturing your body.
Reciting Father Purandaravitthala's holy name
Is the only passport you need to salvation.

Why do you foolishly torture your body,
When you might win merit
By single-mindedly contemplating
The name of Lakshmi's spouse?

Theliso Illa Mulugiso

(Drown Me or Keep Me Afloat)

Drown me or keep me afloat;
I leave it to you,
O my Lord, king of mercy.

I daily bob up and down
In this ocean of life teeming with travail.
Reach me your hand of reassurance,
For my body is frail and my spirit weak.

I have battened on the love of wife and children,
Become addicted to brief human pleasures.
Who but you can rescue me?
Grant that I may touch the hem of your kingly robe.

Mine is the poverty of virtues,
Yours the plenitude of grace.
I slept when I should have prayed,
Laughed when I should have bewept my outcaste state.
Lord Purandaravitthala,
As you recline on your serpent bed,
Grant that I may spend more time
In the company of your devotees.

Drown me or keep me afloat;
I leave it to you,
O my Lord, king of mercy.

Innu Daya Barade Dasana Mele?

(Why Am I Not Worthy of Your Mercy, My Lord?)

Why am I not worthy of your mercy, my Lord,
My Lord Ranga,
You who recline on the sea-serpent?

In many nations,
At different times,
In myriad wombs,
Have I been born and perished.
In each life have I created a hell of me and mine,
But now I know you are my boatman
Across the rough waters of this life.

I kept loyal company with the six deadly sins
Before being baptized by your sacred name.
Lover of Lakshmi, progenitor of the mind,
Have mercy on me.
Your name is my staff.

Thought, word, and deed are all yours even now,
O slayer of demons.
My life is yours,
Let my cry come unto you,
Lord Purandaravitthala,
Lord of boundless mercy.

Why am I not worthy of your mercy, my Lord,
My Lord Ranga,
You who recline on the sea-serpent?

Kandu Kandu Nienna Kay Biduvude Krishna?

(Although You Are Mindful of My Woes)

Although you are mindful of my woes,
Why have you chosen to abandon me?

Kin I have none; I draw each breath in pain.
Crushed am I
By the malice of contumacious men.
My father, mother, kin,
My sole comfort are you, Krishna.

A second becomes an eon, a tittle a mountain
For me in this life of pain-driven worldliness,
Sea-Serpent Lord, lodestar of saints,
Prahlada's protector, Krishna.

People say you are your devotees' present help,
A rock in a weary land.
Prove yourself worthy of that praise,
Grantor of deliverance,
Lord of the City of Or,
All powerful, chief teacher,
Lord Purandaravitthala.

Although you are mindful of my woes,
Why have you chosen to abandon me?

Binnahakke Bayillavayya

(I Have Not the Nerve to Come to You)

I have not the nerve to come to you,
For infinite are my transgressions.
Foe of demons,
The worst of all is forgetting your sacred name.

Love of children,
Love of lust, love of kith and kin,
Love of song, love of royal largesse,
Love of property, love of livestock,
Love of parents
Love of jewelry
Love of precious stones—

Pride in wealth, pride in prestige,
Pride in pre-eminence,
Pride in looks, pride in youth
Pride in fulfillment,
Pride, pride, pride,
More pride.

Getting that, coveting more,
Desiring this man's wealth and that man's wife,
Craving pleasure,
Seeking the ultimate joy, the joy of the senses—
When I know all desire
Except the desire to touch your heavenly feet
Paves the road to hell,
I have not the nerve to come to you,
My Lord Purandaravitthala.

I have not the nerve to come to you,
For infinite are my transgressions.
Foe of demons,
The worst of all is forgetting your sacred name.

Mandamathiyu Nanu

(Muddle-Headed I Am)

Muddle-headed I am,
O father of Kama,
Take not into account my manifold misdeeds.
Protect me.

I am a sinner,
You annihilate sin.
I revel in lust, anger, envy.
You bring peace that passes understanding.
Illusions' child, I,
I look to illusions to bring me to the mirage of peace.

You grant succor to those seeking it;
I travel in search of more damning sins.

An unthinking scarecrow
That bends to every wind am I,
All-knowing protector are you.
Arrogant lord of little knowledge am I,
Greater than the sum
Of the wisdom of the scriptures
Are you.

What if my fortunes are lower than those of the lowest,
Lord of Lakshmi,
Goddess of all wealth?
What if I know not
What is past, present, or to come?
Father Purandaravitthala,
I know you save the least of your servants.

Muddle-headed I am,
O father of Kama,
Take not into account my manifold misdeeds.
Protect me.

Anthakana Dutharige Kinchitthu Dayavilla

(Heralds of Death Have No Mercy)

Waste not nights and days
Quenching lust, thirst, and hunger.
While you are busy with rapine,
Death's clerk keeps track of the moments you forgot Hari.
You never know when his agents come to your door.

You say:
'I just entered matrimony yesterday—
I just bought a new heard of cattle—
I just acquired a large tract of land—
I have gold, women, wine, song—
I am not yet ready to die."
The heralds of death tighten the noose around your worldly neck.

You say to them:
"Don't you see, O Keepers of Time,
I just finished building this house—
I must warm it.
Don't you see,
My wife is about to give birth,
My son about to marry.
Life could not be better."
Heralds of death don't care.
They tighten the noose around your neck.

You tell them:
"Wait, Lords, tomorrow is my new child's christening—
Day after tomorrow is my son's baptism—
Life never had more to offer.
Wait, I am not ready to leave yet."
Heralds of death laugh loudly in the corners of your empty mind.

You tell them:
"I have never had time, my Lords,

To taste the savories lovingly cooked livelong night;
I have never had time to collect my debts.
When darkness began to descend upon me,
I had not time to seek
The light that is Lord Purandaravitthala's name."

Heralds of death don't care.
They tighten the noose around your neck.

Heralds of Death, markers of time, have no mercy.
Worry not about worry, my soul, think on Sri Hari.

Na Madida Karma Balavanthvadare

(Not Even You Can Override My Karma)

Such is the decree of karma that not even you,
Lord of Lords,
Can countermand its effects.
My fate is inscribed on my forehead
By none other than Brahma.

Eating, drinking, and being merry
Took precedence
Over matins, meditation, and evensong.
I had no time for you,
O slayer of demons,
And wandered the world like a dog.

I had no time to offer hospitality to the hungry.
I never could stop lusting after every woman I saw.
Blind desire turned me into an arrant fool.
What's in store for me now,
O eagle-vehicled Krishna?

Execrable sinner that I am,
I still hope for mercy.
Grant me the company of your disciples.
Not one has any kind words for me.
What shall I do,
My Lord Purandaravitthala?

Such is the decree of karma that not even you,
Lord of Lords,
Can countermand its effects.
My fate is inscribed on my forehead
By none other than Brahma.

Aduvamakkalu Maneya Kattidaru

(Children at Play Built a Nice Little House)

Children at play built a nice little house,
When dusk fell, no longer interested in what they had built,
They demolished it.
So must life be, like children's play,
So say the ancient scriptures.

To the market came
Many from many different villages;
When dusk fell,
They left in many directions.

A sparrow flew into the courtyard;
And was gone within a wink.
The lodger arrived at the inn,
And left before sunrise.

If you want to break the bonds
Of this impermanent life,
Pray to Lord Purandaravitthala,
The slayer of Kamsa.

Children at play built a nice little house,
When dusk fell, no longer interested in what they had built,
They demolished it.
So must life be, like children's play,
So say the ancient scriptures.

Kallusakkare Kolliro

(Accept this Hard Candy)

My friends, come on,
Accept this piece of hard candy.

Not all can enjoy this sugar crystal,
But those who know the name of Lotus-Eyed Sri Krishna.

This is no commodity carted off to the market
On the backs of dumb beasts,
Nor is this something packed
As tightly as possible into sacks to save space.
No matter where you take it, it is not taxed.
There is no other thing on the market
Which can bring as much profit as this sugar crystal,
Much in demand everywhere.

Never have you to worry about cutting your losses;
Never does this sugar crystal decay and rot.
Ants come nowhere near it.
It needs no loud advertising, either.

This sugar crystal is never carried
From marketplace to marketplace,
Nor does transporting it fatigue one.
It forever sweetens the tongues of the devotees.
It is called Purandaravitthala,
The unperturbed one.

My friends, come on,
Accept this piece of hard candy.

Narayananemba Namada Byjava

(Plant the Seed Called Narayana)

Fellow cultivators,
Let's plant the seed named Narayana
On the tip of our tongues.

Let us turn our hearts into fields,
Let our minds be ploughshares,
Let our lungs be the twin bulls,
Kept in control
By the leash of knowledge.
Let us drop the seed in furrows called selflessness.

Let us weed
The field of lust and anger.
Let us cast
A net to catch the birds of distraction.

Two measures I see,
Birth and death.
What sinful measures come between the two before harvest,
Lord Purandaravitthala turns into chaff and blows away

Fellow cultivators,
Let's plant the seed named Narayana
On the tip of our tongues.

Adahodalle Makkalu

(Children Tease Me at Play, Mommy)

Children tease me at play, Mommy,
And I am sick of it.
They look at me and make faces.

I am a foundling,
They say, son of Devaki.
Somebody called Vasudeva is my father,
They say.
Born in a mean manger,
They say.
To save me from my murderous uncle they brought me here,
The children say.

They say I killed the she-demon
Whose breasts were filled with poison.
They say I killed a demon
Disguised as a cartwheel.

They taunt me,
Saying you are not my birth mother.
They say I am here because you needed one more cowherd.
They say your love for me has no bounds.

Oh, yes, they say I swallowed the poison
Of a king cobra sent to kill me.

They make fun of my humble possessions.
The eagle is my cart,
The serpent my bed.
Furthermore, they say I am a thief,
Stealing butter from their houses
Like lovely little Purandaravitthala.

Children tease me at play, Mommy,
And I am sick of it.
They look at me and make faces.

Kelano Hari Talano

(Take My Word for it, Hari Has No Time for this Music)

Take my word for it,
Our Lord Hari has no time for this kind of music.
It has rhythm, melody, and beat,
But no love.

In heaven, the muses sing to Hari;
They are accompanied by stringed instruments and tambourines.
There is not a note they cannot sound,
Not a key they miss.
Our Lord is sung to by those loftiest musicians,
Narada and Thumburu.
Why do you impostors imagine he will listen
To your cachinnation of hypocrisy?

For Hari, there is a multiplicity of tunes, tones, and pitches,
Each according to the sentiment of the follower.
His very name is music;
Cheap literary embellishments merit not his attention.

If you want to sing to Lord Hari,
Forget all the rules.
Fill your hearts with love instead of figures of speech.
Sing along with his true followers.
Lord Purandaravitthala will listen
Regardless of pitch, tone, or melody.

Take my word for it,
Our Lord Hari has no time for this kind of music.

Nambu Kandya Manave

(Trust, My Mind, Sri Krishna's Holy Feet)

Trust, my soul,
Sri Krishna's holy feet.

This city with its nine openings
Is not impregnable.
Don't celebrate its temporary glory.

Six thieves are out there,
Waiting to plunder the city.

This seven layered fortress
Is not formidable to the heralds of death.

Don't you understand?
This body, sustained though it is through
The power of God,
Is helpless against the onslaught of the Heralds of Death?

Don't hope to inhabit this town, this body, forever.
While you still can,
Allow your mind to be filled
With the vision of our Lord Purandaravitthala's holy feet.

Trust, my soul,
Sri Krishna's holy feet.

Dasana Madiko Enna

(Allow Me to Be Your Serf)

Allow me to be your serf,
Have you not tried me long enough,
My Lord of infinite mercy?

Strip me of sinful tendencies;
Cover my heart with your buckler of mercy.
Let me worship you at your feet,
And place the flower of your reassurance on my head.

Steady meditation of you is all I crave;
I daily offer my respect to your divine feet.
Why do you look at me out of the corner of your eye
And ignore me?
Cleanse my heart,
Teach it to adore you.

You are famous for rescuing
Those who beg you for help.
My sins are countless.
Obliterate them, my Lord Purandaravitthala.

Allow me to be your serf,
Have you not tried me long enough,
My Lord of infinite mercy?

Bandanene Ranga, Bandanene?

(I Want to Know If My Lord Ranga Is About)

Tell me, if my Lord Ranga is about.
Ranga, my child,
My father, purloiner of butter.

Imagine the tintinnabulation of those gold anklets,
My girlfriend.
Think of those resplendent feet.
Doesn't our Krishna,
Resting on that leaf, outshine the world?

His bracelets jingle, jingle, jingle, jingle,
The little bells on his belt tinkle, tinkle, tinkle.
His dancing feet extract
A rhythmic movement from the floor.

"Go, get him,"
"Go, get that plunderer of our hearts,"
Say the desperate milkmaids.
He skips, he trips, and says,
"Catch me!"
When caught,
Our Lord Purandaravitthala says,
"Sweethearts, please let me go."
And we do.

Tell me, if my Lord Ranga is about.
Ranga, my child, my father,
Purloiner of butter.

Bhagyada Lakshmi

(Goddess of Plenty)

Bhagyada Lakshmi,
Let your feet walk this way.
Step after step,
Let the tinkling of your anklet.
Come to my home
When it is time to worship decent people and saints.
Appear to me like a ball of butter in buttermilk.

Come, mother,
Showering gold,
Teach my mind to win what it wants.
Come, Janaka's daughter,
O you, whose brilliance is unmatched by a million suns.

Do not look this way or that.
Let it be always feast and celebration
In your devotees' homes.
You who shine in the liberated minds of decent people,
Doll of gold,
Let your feet walk this way.

Grant me wealth that does not decay.
Bless me with your braceleted hands,
O Lotus-eyed one, bedecked with kumkum
O Venkataramana's bewitching bride.

River of ghee and sugar,
In time for Friday evening's worship
Loving, Alagiri Ranga's,
Purandaravitthala's beloved queen,
Bhagyada Lakshmi,
Let your feet walk this way.

Nindakarirabeku

(May Calumniators Prosper)

May calumniators prosper.
As swine keep a street clean by devouring filth,
So calumniators reduce my burden of sin,
While those who praise me
Steal my accumulated merit.

Evil men are needed in this world,
For they make the good visible.
Grantor of all desires,
Sri Krishna, hear my supplication.

May calumniators prosper.
Aren't they too objects of your scorn,
My lord Purandaravitthala?

May calumniators prosper.

Naneke Badavanu, Naneke Paradeshi?

(Why Do People Say I Am Poor and Homeless?)

Why do people say
I am poor and homeless,
Hari, Lord of all,
When I have you by my side?

You are my eight kin,
My closest friend.
You are the eight jewels in my safe.
How am I poor and homeless my lord,
Form of forms,
When I have you by my side?

You are my siblings,
You are my provider.
You clothe me,
You keep me warm, my lord.
You will not allow my wife and children to perish.
Not for a moment do you forget us,
I know, my lord.

You are my teacher,
You are my guide,
The only one who can lead me to salvation.
Lying by your feet,
Why would I fear anything?
Why do people say
I am poor and homeless,
My lord, Father Purandaravitthala?

Aru Hithavaru Ninage I Muvarolage?

(Who Among these Three Will Come to Your Aid?)

Who among these three will come to your aid?
The fleshpot, the tyrant, or endless wealth?

Marrying out of your caste,
You brought this woman home,
To be its mistress.
She, your inseparable other half,
Now just won't look you in the eye,
For fear of being found out.

On land ruled by a million kings before,
You decreed a stately mansion.
Fortified it with turrets and cannon sites.
You dug a trench around it.
When your breath stops,
Your exquisite body
Will rot in the sun until cremated or buried.

Don't trust this impermanent shell.
Don't squander your time on earthly things.
Remember,
The one undying power in the world is Lord Purandaravitthala.

Praise him
While you still can and be blessed.

Dharmakke Kay Baradi Kala

(This Is No Time for Good People)

In evil time the good perish
While the evil prosper.
Men lack the strength
To resist temptation.

Backstabbers, vicious lawbreakers prosper.
Righteous wives and innocent children starve.

O yes, prostitutes mint money.
Their pimps are in charge of everything.

The holy man and the mendicant are disdained.

Adultery, lying, thieving
Are the gods people whore after.

Servants, viragos rule the roost.
Aging mothers are on the street.

Falsehood is truth, truth falsehood.
No one, none, cares
To meditate on Lord Purandaravitthala's name.

Enu Madidarenu Bhava Hingadu

(The World Is Too Much with Us)

I cannot free myself, no,
From my addiction to this painful life,
O, slayer of demons,
Unless you have mercy on me.

I have performed matins
Long before sunrise;
I have scrubbed my body
In the cold river water;
I have lain prostrate before idols.
I have not much strength left.

Lord, have mercy on me.

I have read the scriptures
From beginning to end,
Over and over.
The exercise has dimmed my sight.
I have bruised my body by endless penance.
O, father of Kama,
Have mercy on me.

I have given alms;
I have taken a vow of silence,
Hoping for that ultimate prize, moksha.

Unless you, Purandaravitthala,
Guardian of orphans,
Have mercy on me,
I cannot free myself, no,
From my addiction to this painful life.

Karuniso Ranga

(Grant Me Lord Ranga)

Lord Ranga,
Grant that I may never cease to recite your holy name,
By the second, the minute, the hour, and the day.

A poor man, I have no gifts to bring.
I cannot vow to be singing your praise like Rukumangada,
Nor am I renowned for giving gifts like the foe of Baka.
I am no match for Devaki in loving you.

Lord Ranga,
Grant I may never cease to recite your holy name.

I am not Garuda, bearing you
On his back across the universe,
Nor do I know how to draw you
To this earth like the king of elephants.
I cannot serve you like the honorable monkey,
Nor can I please you like Lakshmi.

I am not Bali,
gifting away his empire.
I am not Prahlada,
Whose tears washed your feet.
I am not Arjuna, your comrade-in-arms.
Watch over me, God of gods,
Purandaravitthala.

Lord Ranga,
Grant that I may never cease to recite your holy name,
By the second, the minute, the hour, and the day.

Manava Janma Doddadu

(Human Life Is Precious)

Human life is precious,
O ye foolish men.
Don't throw it away.
Why use your hands, feet, eyes, and ears
To grab a handful of dirt and eat it?
Grasping at women and wealth,
Why be hungry
By failing to meditate on Hari?

As heralds of death lasso you in,
If you say,
 "Please wait, O please wait!"
What do they care?

Take advantage of being human;
Sing Lord Hari's praise.
Garner merit.

If you forget Krishna the cowherd's name,
Children, wealth, and status
Are nothing when you take that last breath.

Before you take that last breath,
Enjoy your humanity.
Be blessed.
Twist your tongue and say,
"Purandaravitthala!"

Human life is precious,
O ye foolish men.
Don't throw it away.

Naranada Mele Harinama Jihweylirabeku

(To Be Human Is to Let Hari's Name Forever Be on One's Tongue)

To be human is to let Hari's name
Forever be on one's tongue.
To be human is
To be kind to all creatures,
To try to be sinless,
To chant Hari's name nonstop.

To be human is
To transcend the six deadly sins,
To cross the three qualities,
To be part of godhead.

To be human is
To subdue the eight manifestations of pride,
To eschew the company of the wicked,
To say, "Krishna, Keshava" nonstop.

To be human is
To study the Vedas,
To give up pride in one's birth,
To sing Madhava's praise forever.

To be human is
To offer peace, kindness, and mercy,
To keep anger and delusion away,
To associate with the godly.

To be human is
To worship the guru's feet,
To follow the way of renunciation,
To happily eat what one has,
To take blame and praise in stride, and
To glorify the name of Lord Purandaravitthala.

Kusanu Kandira?

(Have You Seen this Holy Child?)

Have you seen this Holy Child?

This Holy Child shines like a billion suns together;
This Holy Child is worshipped under a million names.

This Holy Child hands out imperishable knowledge;
This Holy Child proffers the joy that knows no attrition.

This Holy Child's playground is the ocean of enlightenment;
This Holy Child is effulgent in the hearts of those who know.

This Holy Child is easily accessible to the lowest of his serfs.
This Holy Child is aware of his own inexplicable splendor.

This Holy Child surveys the tripartite world;
This Holy Child is formless in spite of his form.

This Holy Child is invisible to those lost in the world;
This Holy Child is resident in thought, word, and deed.

This Holy Child is out of the reach of those proud of their paltry knowledge.
Our Holy Child is none other than Lord Purandaravitthala Himself.

Have you seen this Holy Child?

Donku Balada Nayakare

(O My Lord of the Wagging Tail)

What did you dine on today,
O my lord of the wagging tail?

I guess you enjoyed visiting the rice-threshing room,
Looking at the business through the window.
Did your lordship enjoy singing
When you were whacked with the thresher?

Was your lordship led to the kitchen
By the sweet smell of the rice pudding?
Did your lordship enjoy singing
When your tail received a thwacking from the ladle?

Were the odorific alleys to your lordship's liking?
Please tell your servant
What joy it was to roll in dust and ashes behind the kitchen.

As long as your lordship deigns to forget Purandaravitthala,
Your daily routine shall remain the same.

Kayalareno Krishna Kandavara Bagilanu

(Enough of this Hanging by People's Doorsteps, Krishna)

Enough of this hanging by people's doorsteps, Krishna,
Like an abandoned puppy,
Yapping at their heels.

Enough of not glorifying you
On waking up in the morning,
Enough of trotting
Around worthless humans' houses,
Enough of waiting for their offal.

It is not impossible
To liquify stone,
Not impossible to extract oil
From dry peas.
But it is impossible
To please the scorner's heart,
Although I beg, plead, and grovel,
With all my teeth on show.

Caught in the net of soul-destroying desires,
Illusion's child, I know not
How or when this torture will end.
Release me from error and worry,
Lord Purandaravitthala.

Enough of this hanging by people's doorsteps, Krishna,
Like an abandoned puppy,
Yapping at their heels.

Yarige Yaruntu Eravina Samsara

(This Life Is a Debt Owed in Previous Incarnations)

What is anybody to anybody
In this life,
A debt owed in previous lives?
How long does a water bubble last, O Hari?

No sooner I reached
Into a well to end tongue-drying thirst
Did the water evaporate away.

No sooner I stood under a tree
To get away from the blinding sun in hot air
Did the tree collapse on top of my head.

No sooner did I build a cradle in the woods
Did my infant disappear.

My end, too,
Is near.
Watch over me,
Hari, Lord Purandaravitthala.

Kottavaru Sariye, Kodade Biitavaru Sariye

(We Love All, the Stingy and the Generous)

We love all, the stingy and the generous.

What matters if the stingy kick us out
And the generous set a rich table for us?
Nothing matters to us,
The devotees of the demon-slayer Krishna.

We are at home with beggars and emperors.
The clown and the calumniator
Matter not to us,
Worshipers of Krishna's lotus feet.

Our progenitor is the king of kings.
Lord Purandaravitthala,
Who stands atop the hill,
Is our provider,
Forever and a day.

Nageyu Baruthide Enage, Nageyu Baruthide

(These Clowns Crack Me Up)

God, what a sight these mortals are!
These clowns crack me up.

They covet their neighbors' wives.
Sometimes they lie with them.
And then they stand
In the middle of a stream for hours,
Rebaptizing themselves.

There are women,
Who lie with men other than their husbands.
They fast, they pray.
These goody two-shoes crack me up.

Look at that holy caricature.
Tells others to shed the six deadly sins.
His own heart is filled with them.
He recites your holy name,
My lord Purandaravitthala.

These clowns crack me up.

Nambadiru I Deha Nithyavalla

(Trust Not this Shell, the Body)

Hey, you poor fool,
Trust not this shell, the body.
Meditate on the Lotus-Eyed One.

What is this body
But bones, blood, and flesh covered by
A blanket of skin?
A mere container of urine and excrement,
It is home to sickness and filth.

Get beyond the material body and its tricks.
Don't destroy your soul
By endlessly consorting with wife, wealth, and children.
There is a tomorrow in a different world.

Don't waste time badmouthing others.
Don't waste time
Coveting your neighbor's wife or daughter.
Respect your elders and teachers.

Trust not this shell, the body,
But only Purandaravitthala's holy name.

Idu Bhagya, Idu Bhagyvayya

(What Greater Happiness Can There Be?)

What greater happiness can there be,
Than blessing the Lotus-Naveled One's joyous name?

There is no greater happiness
Than being a stone in the midst of the rough stream of life,
Than submitting to the wisdom of the learned,
Than silently cultivating Madhava's grace,
Than being happy with friends and relatives.

There is no greater happiness
Than constantly righting one's mind and body,
Than being in the grace of the devout,
Than studying guru Madhwa's tenets,
Than being pure in thought, word, and deed.

There is no greater happiness
Than keeping the desire of the flesh under control,
Than glorifying Lord Hari day and night,
Than serving the serfs of Purandaravitthala.

What greater happiness can there be,
Than blessing the Lotus-Naveled One's joyous name?

Na Ninna Dhyanadoliralu

(If I Am Meditating on You)

If I am meditating on you,
What harm can mean humans wreak on me,
O Gopala?
Your name is my buckler
Against their envy and hatred.
If I am thinking of you,
I am a fire untroubled by driver ants.

If a horse take it into his head
To dance in the wind,
Can the dust kicked up by him touch the sun?
Say, what can trouble the minds of your devotees?
Can a wayward breeze shake a mountain?

Can a thief steal the pot of gold he spies in a mirror?
Do not doubt my faith.
Watch over me, Purandaravitthala,
Whose resting place is a serpent.

If I am meditating on you,
What harm can mean humans wreak on me,
O Gopala?
Your name is my shield against their envy and hatred.

Ninyako Ninna Hangyako?

(Why Do I Need You, if I Am Girded by Your Holy Name?)

Why do I need you, if I am girded by your sacred name?
There is no bulwark like your name.

When the King of Elephants
Had his leg in the jaws of the crocodile,
What saved him but your name, "Adimula?"

When Draupadi
Was about to be raped,
What rescued her
But your sacred name, "Krishna?"

When Little Dhruva
Sobbed for you in the forest,
What comforted him
But your name, "Vasudeva?"

When Yama's heralds
Were putting a noose around
Ajamila's neck,
What saved him
But your name "Narayana?"

What do I care
If you don't care about me?

Your name alone,
Lord Purandaravitthala
Is my shield against trouble.

Madhava Nina Murutiyane Nililso

(Lord Madhava, Let My Eyes Always Feast on Your Divine Form)

Lord Madhava,
Let my eyes always feast on your divine form.

Let me always envision that garland of tender basil around your neck.
Let me always envision your divine form
Attired in that splendid yellow gold cloth.
Lord Madhava,
Let my eyes always feast on your divine form.
Let me always envision your neck garlanded
By the nine stones and diamond-glinted ring finger;
Let me always envision your noble head resting
On Lakshmi's necklaced breasts.
Lord Madhava,
Let my eyes always feast on your divine form.

O supplicants' clear and present help,
Their unfailing grantor of wishes,
Provider of deliverance,
Purandaravitthala,
The tree of plenty,
Let my eyes always feast on your divine form.

Lord Madhava,
Let my eyes always feast on your divine form.

Yadava Ni Ba

(O Yadava, Let Us See You)

O Yadava, hope of the Yadu clan, let us see you.
You who slew your evil uncle in Madhure,
Son of Yashoda, let us see you.

Your anklets tinkling,
Your bracelets jingling,
Playing in the company of those urchins,
Let's have a glimpse of you.

Adorned with the conch and the wheel,
You let us have a glimpse of your loveliness;
You, unblemished being of greatness,
Adinarayana,
Let us, your devotees, have a glimpse of you.

O rider of the eagle,
God in myriad forms,
My lord of the everlasting smile,
Let us have a glimpse of you.
I will sing your praise all over the world.

O Purandaravitthala,
Let's have a glimpse of you.

O Yadava, the hope of the Yadu clan, let us see you.
You who slew thy evil uncle in Madhure,
Son of Yashoda, let us see you.

Tarakka Bindige Na Nirige Hoguve

(My Sister, Grab that Earthen Pot)

My sister, grab that pot.
Let's go fetch some of the sweetest water in this world
Flowing in that stream.
Hurry sister, grab that pot.
Don't worry if it breaks, as you grab it.
It costs only a penny.
The name of the stream is Rama.
Let's fill the pot with that holy name.
Many of our friends are already there,
But there is plenty of this holy water for us all.
Come on, let's go to that stream,
Flowing round the temple.
Let's collect the water
And use it to wash the feet
Of our Lord Purandaraviththala.
My sister, grab that pot.

Krishna Enabarade Omme

(Say Krishna Once in a While!)

Say Krishna once in a while!
Watch your troubles fade away
While you are still in possession
Of this valuable human life.

While you still have a tongue,
Say Krishna once in a while!

As you stretch, as you yawn,
As you walk through the house,
Say Krishna once in a while!

As you pray, bathe, meditate,
As you dine and belch,
Say Krishna once in a while!

As you carry a heavy load,
As you seek to find your way,
Say once in a while,
Lord of Dwaraka,
Purandaravitthala indeed is Krishna!

Say Krishna once in a while!
Watch your troubles fade away.

Jagaduddharana Adisidalu Yashode

(Yashoda Keeps Her Divine Child Occupied)

Yashoda keeps her divine child occupied.
Yashoda entertains the savior of the world.
The Lord of Lords is her child.

The essence of the universe is her child,
Yashoda entertains her divine child.
He who is beyond the scriptures,
He whose miracles cannot be counted,
That jewel of children is her child.
Yashoda entertains her divine child.

He who is smaller than the atom,
He who is larger than the universe,
The unmade maker,
He who is everywhere is her child.
Yashoda entertains her divine child.

He who is the Supreme Being,
He who is the son Vasudeva
He who is Purandaravitthala is her child

Yashoda keeps her divine child occupied.
Yashoda entertains the savior of the world.

Gudu Sikkalilla, Gudina Jadu Thiliyalilla

(Never Reached Home)

Never reached home,
Never knew how to get there.

Now my two wives have run away.
The walls of my house have collapsed,
Leaving an empty square behind.

Never learned to be careful,
Never snapped out of my arrogance.

I have watched my lumps of sugar
Fall into the fire and melt in madness.

I am old now;
Did not chew nice food when I could.
My pot of honey has fallen
On a mound of refuse.

I've spent all my merit,
Don't know what next.

Why didn't I think
To fill my empty heart
With the sweet name of Lord Purandaravitthala?

Never reached home,
Never knew how to get there.

Gummana Kareyadire, Amma Ninu

(Please Don't Summon the Bogeyman, Mother)

Please don't summon the bogeyman, mother.
I will be quiet, won't grab at your breasts,
I will drink my milk and be quiet.

I will leave those maidens alone.
I promise not to cover their eyes with my hands.
I won't bully anyone, won't bug my brother.

I will not steal butter anymore, nor will I eat mud.
I won't scare you by sitting on the edge of the well.
Never will I touch a snake again.

I won't free the calves so they can drink up all the milk.
I will sit still in a comer, like a god.

Hearing the crafty words of her little son,
Gopidevi, smiling
Embraces the savior of the world,
Lord Purandaravitthala.

Yare Rangana, Yare Krishnana?

(Who Is at the Door?)

Who is at the door,
Asking our Ranga,
Our Krishna, to come out and play?

Who calls to Gopalakrishna, destroyer of sins,
In this manner, at this hour?
Who wants to disturb our flawless flutist,
Our love, the darling of lovely maidens?

Who is at the door,
Calling the one who saved the Elephant King?

Who is at the door,
Seeking our Lord Purandaravitthala,
The Supreme Being?

Who is at the door,
Asking our Ranga, our Krishna,
To come out and play?

Kagada Bandide

(A Letter Has Arrived)

A letter has arrived from the lotus-naveled one.
Renounce lust and anger, says the letter.

Say your prayers, do right things at the right time, says the letter.
Waste not your time with godless wastrels, says the letter.
And the letter is from the father of Kama.

Do not squander precious time chasing women, says the letter.
Do not waste holy time coveting land, says the letter.

Do not fritter away sacred time desiring gold, says the letter.
And the letter is from none other than the husband of Lakshmi,
Goddess of all wealth.

Wear your anklets proudly, says the letter.
Dance with joy says, the letter.

Recite Hari's name loudly and proudly at every step, says the letter,
And the letter is personally written by our Lord Purandaravitthala.

A letter has arrived from the Lotus-Naveled One.

Hariya Neneyiro Namma

(Sing Our Hari's Praise)

Sing our Hari's praise,
Sing our Hari's praise;
Let not your mouths become deserts of barren words.

This temporary abode, the body,
Is even more evanescent than you think.
Don't throw away that precious commodity, time.
Time's winged chariot is always hurrying near.

Shed lust and anger, memorize the story of the father of Kama.
Recite that story again and again with love.
Do these, and you will escape the fate of the riff-raff.

If your feet tread the land traveled by Hari,
Your sins will cease to follow you.
Touch the feet of Hari
And sing the praise of the emperor of emperors,
Purandaravitthala.

Sing our Hari's praise,
Sing our Hari's praise;
Let not your mouths become deserts of barren words.

Nire Ni Karethare

(O Wandering Maiden, Won't You Summon Our Handsome Lord?)

Won't you Summon our Blue-skinned, handsome lore?
O swaying sprightly maiden,
Won't you summon our blue-skinned handsome lord?
Won't you usher in our beautiful blue-skinned, lovely lord?

O swaying sprightly maiden,
Won't you find for us the stealer of butter from cowherds' cottages?
Won't you find for us that little rascal?

O swaying sprightly maiden,
Won't you summon for us your paramour,
The love of our lives, that mesmerizing flutist?

O happy, sprightly maiden,
Won't you bring in our sweetheart Purandaravitthala for a second?

O wandering, sprightly maiden,
Won't you summon our blue-skinned handsome lord?
Won't you usher in our beautiful blue-skinned, lovely lord?

Duru Maduvarene?

(I Have Had Enough of Their Complaints)

I have had enough of their complaints,
Of these wanton wives and daughters of our cowherds.

They call my child a thief of butter.
Don't the fools know my little Ranga
Shines love on heaven, earth, and hell?
The cows and calves follow him to the village pasture,
Finding his fluting irresistible.

The shameless wives and daughters say
He enters their houses on the way
And steals kisses from them.
I have had enough of their complaints.

Why can't they be honest
And admit they cannot help being aroused
By the beauty of my baby and Lord
Purandaravitthala?

I have had enough of their complaints,
Of these wanton wives and daughters of our cowherders.

Bandaddella Barali

(Come What May, I Care Not)

Come what may, I care not,
As long as Govinda is watching over me,
If Indiraramana resides in my mind,
I need fear no evil.

Evil Kaurava trapped his cousins, the Pandavas,
In a house wax and gloated as he set fire to it.
The fire touched not a hair of the Pandavas,
For our Hari lived in their hearts and minds.

What matters if people despise me,
 If you are on my side, O slayer of demons?
Let troubles come in hordes.

What power had Yama ever over your devotees, Hari?
He who rides the lion need never fear the elephant.
He who lives in Ranga's blessing is never engulfed by the mortal world's torture.

Blessed Lord of abundant mercy,
Purandaravitthala,
I need fear no evil .

As long as you are on my side.
Come what may, I care not.

Allide Namma Mane

(My Home Is over There)

My home is over there;
I am visiting this one
Out of mere curiosity.
The portal of this house leads
To pain disguised as pleasure.
Vaikuntha, the abode of our Lotus-Naveled Lord,
Is my true home.

Don't be complacent
About owning your two-storey house.
Sing Hari's praise; serve his serfs.
When Yama's merciless henchmen show up without notice,
Will they pause to admire your impermanent dwelling?
Your lovely children, beautiful wife, friends in this house
Will not accompany you on that final journey.

Earn a space in the divine realm
Of our Lord Purandaravitthala
By living righteously in this home.

My home is over there;
I am visiting this one
Out of mere curiosity.
Out of mere curiosity.

Arenu Maduvaru Avaniyolage?

(What Avails One, When Karma)

What avails one,
When karma dogs him every step of the way?

If the food spoil as soon as it is cooked,
If the husband disappear,
If the wife turn the marital bed into a torture chamber,
If the tiger painted on the wall come to life,
If words one never uttered be held against him,
If the fence eat its charges, if the rabbit kill the catcher,
If one's one own hand crack one's head open when scratching it,
If the ponytail turn into a serpent, if friend become foe,
If the rice on the platter turn into shards when put in the mouth,
If the mother suckle her children with poison,
If the father sell his children on the market,
If the servant bark orders at the master,
If darkness turn into a clawing bear,
If the doll's reflection in the eyeball bite,
If the wife do nothing but fight,
If indigestion plague a hungry wretch,
If baptism in a holy river compound one's sins,
If the tree-branch one is resting on break in twain,
If fate swallow luck,
If charcoal catch fire on its own when held in the palm,
Then, my lord Purandaravitthala,
If you are not there,
What avails one,
When karma dogs him every step of the way?

Gudgudinnu Sedi Nodo

(Try this Hubble-Bubble)

Try this hubble-bubble,
And forget your trouble.
Let those gut-deep sins be exhaled.

Let the smoke unseal that bag, your mind,
And scatter the daily collection of skins.
Let the intoxication
Pass through the tube of the body,
And start the fire called Krishna.

Your skull the gourd—
Your faith in your guru the tube—
Narayana the cooling water.
Come on, take a pull on this hubble-bubble.

Takes no time to feel high.
All forms of poverty flee through the nostrils
Like stale smoke.
The mind then has a vision
Of our Lord Purandaravitthala.

Kendake Warale Muthuvudunte?

(Have You Ever Seen Wasps Attack Live Coals?)

Have you ever seen wasps attack live coals,
Or Ranga's dasas become afraid of life?

Where is the elephant making friends with the lion,
Where the street dog cavorting with the tiger?

Where is the man singing Hari's praise
And tortured by poverty?

Can darkness envelop the sun?
Can the tree frog swallow the snake in his hole?

Where is the boxer who hurt his hand
By punching the air?

Where is he who worships our Purandaravitthala
And fears hell?

Huvva Tharuvara Manege Hulla Tharuva

(Offer Our Lord a Flower, He'll Feed Your Livestock with Grass)

Offer our Lord a flower.
You can be sure
He will bring grass for your livestock grass.
Our lord doesn't mind being our servant.

A single leaf of basil,
A single drop from the Ganga,
A moment of devotion—
He needs no more to be your servant.

The Pandavas were His devotees.
He scrubbed their horses,
Fed them straw.

Our Lord Purandararavitthala
Is the slave of His slaves.

Nanu Bera Maduve

(This Is My Trade)

This is my trade.

I ride my tongue, the bull.
I fill my body, the sack,
With grain called Rama.

When toll collectors, the five senses,
Stop me,
I immobilize them with the seal
Of Krishna.

I sell unwavering faith
In my lord Purandaravitthala.
Salvation is my assured profit.

This is my trade.

Ambiga Na Ninna Nambide

(Boatman, You Are My Hope)

Boatman, you are my hope.
Spouse of the world's mother,
You are my hope.

This boat is crowded.
It is punctured in nine places.
Don't desert me.
Direct it.

The river rages.
The rapids run deep.
The currents swirl me in.
Pull me out, boatman.

Look at those six rough waves.
Who can slow them down but you?
Boatman, you are my hope.

Boatman, my time is past.
Look at those five enemies of mine.
Oar me past them;
Lead me to the land of peace.

Boatman, paddle my boat in the right path.
What is dark in me, illumine.
Oar me to the temple of salvation,
Where resides my Lord Purandaravitthala.

Boatman, you are my hope.

Rama Rama Rama Rama Rama Enniro

(Say Rama, Rama, Rama, Rama, Rama)

Say Rama, Rama, Rama, Rama, Rama.
Daily breathe that holy name.

This crowded city has nine gates.
Its proud rulers are five in number.
Don't be fooled by their tinsel splendor.
Don't throw your lives away doing their bidding.

This scaffold of bones,
Covered with skin,
Hides flesh, urine, and feces.

This scarecrow in the field of life
Dances to the tune of transient desires.
You own it for a minute.

Wife, children, family are no jewels.
Don't sport them.
When Death says, "Come,"
Nobody hears the summons but you.

There is a sure way to salvation.
Sing the praise of our Purandaravitthala,
King of Kings and God of Gods.

Nayi Bandadappa, Anna, Aththalagiri

(Spurn this Dog, Brothers)

Spurn this dog, brothers.
This is no ordinary pariah dog,
But a cur in human form.

This mangy dog paid no debts,
Kept no promise.
Yet he sits on the porch,
Lording it over little curs.

Shares a bone,
But is full of jealousy.
Still in the mother-bitch's womb,
Lusted after siblings.

Deserts his consort,
Whoring after loose bitches.

This cur had a chance,
But never once worshipped
Our lord Purandaravitthala.

Spurn this dog, brothers.

Kaunakara Ninembuvyadyathako, Bharaavasavillenege

(Why Pretend with the Rest You Are Merciful?)

Why pretend with the rest
That you are merciful?
I know no such thing.

You put me through the mill
Of this human life
And crush my heart everyday.

Oh yes, I know all about those legends.
You came to the aid of Bali, Panchali, and Ahalye.
When I think about those myths,
They are no more than a bunch of make-believe.

Is it true that you are merciful?
All right, come, hold my hand now.
O Lotus-Eyed One,
Prove to me I don't need to bother
With mundane worries.

They tell me you saved
Ajamila on his deathbed.
If you want to protect
Your reputation as the eagle-flagged savior,
Lord Purandaravitthala,
Help me now.

Why pretend with the rest
You are merciful?
I know no such thing.

Yake Kakulath Paduve Ele Marule?

(Why Do You Fret, My Poor Soul?)

Why do you fret, my poor soul?

How hard it can be for our lord
Who rules the three worlds
To watch over a few mortals?

He feeds the frog in the cleft of the rock.
He brings succor to the hermit in the forest.
He won't forget you.

Who creates seed, weed, and leaf
For the creatures of the wild?
He feeds the bird that swings from branch to branch.

Millions of life forms
Draw sustenance from Him.
Trust in our lord Purandaravitthala.

Why do you fret, my poor soul?

Kage Ka Ennali Hariye

(Let the Crows Caw, Hari)

Let the crows caw, Hari.
Let the songbirds sing their symphony.
Let the kokila stream the sky with her song.
Let the champaks sweetly bloom, my baby.

Up, up, wash your face.
Let me adorn your forehead with tilaka.
Pats of fresh butter wait on a platter
For you, baby.
The blanket of darkness is folded back by light.
It's time to wake up, my baby.

I will serve you hot pancakes,
With sweet yogurt on the side.
Yes, there will also be perfumed rice
Seasoned with brown sugar and spice.

Why are you trying my patience
This morning, my sweet child?

Who but I will hold you, Lord of Lords,
My divine child, Purandaravitthala?

Huchu Hidiyithu Enage Huchu Hidiyithu

(I Have Gone Plum Crazy)

I have gone plum crazy.
I am drunk with the name Krishna.

I will run through the streets,
Screaming, "Vasudeva!"

I will rend my shirt called sin.
Pull my hair out
Along with the lice of sin
Embedded in it.

I will kick at every wall
That stands between me and God.

I will circle the righteous,
Even as I fling stones at the wicked.

I will make faces at the soul-less,
Even as I sling dirt at those
Who calumniate my lord Hari.

I will dance in frenzy
To whatever tune
My friends,
Purandaravitthala's devotees play.

I have gone plum crazy.

Ni Kode Na Bide Kelayya Matha

(I Will Not Stop Dogging You)

I will not stop dogging you.
You owe me big time,
Lord of Gokula, Govinda.

What is to stop me
From glorifying you?
Cut out your playfulness.
Shell out the interest
On my devotion.

The principal of devotion can't be written off.
I demand interest on the words
I use about you.

The pleasures of this life
Are no payment.
The deed is quit
When you grant me salvation,
My lord Purandaravitthala.

I will not stop dogging you.

Ena Pelele Gopi Ninna Magana Jala

(O Mother of Krishna)

"O mother of Krishna,
How can I describe your child's mischief?

Your shameless child
Sneaked into my kitchen.

Drank the milk;
Broke the milkpots.
Hid in a big one.

I caught him.
How could I beat him?
Is our Lord a worthless urchin?

Joined my daughter in her room
Looking exactly like my son-in-law.
Said he was going to leave her.
To humor him, I allowed him to stay.
Now my daughter is no longer chaste."

O women of the village, don't wrong my child.
The world's maker, my baby.
Look, Lord Purandaravitthala,
Is sound asleep."

Notes:

p. 3
Brahma: Creator of the universe, second of the Hindu trinity, the other two being ***Vishnu*** and ***Shiva***

p.*4*
Udupi: a pilgrimage center in South India where a temple was erected to Krishna in the early fifteenth century

p.*5*
Hari *is one of the many names of* ***Krishna***

p.*6*
Dasa means serf of ***Krishna***. **Nama** is a vertical mark worn on the forehead by dasas.

p.*7*
Ajamila : A sinner saved serendipitously when, dying, he called upon his son ***Narayana***, which also happens to be one of ***Krishna***'s many names.

p. *9*
Sea-Serpent: Vishnu's bed is the nine-headed ***Shesha***. **Ranga** is one of the names of ***Vishnu***, very popular among his devotees in South India. The six deadly sins are: Envy, lust, jealousy, hatred, anger, and gluttony.

p. *10*
Kama is the Hindu god of sexual love. ***Vishnu*** is his father. ***Lakshmi***, the goddess of wealth is Vishnu's spouse. His other spouse is the goddess of earth, ***Bhudevi***.

p. *15*
In Hindu mythology ***Karma*** is the sum total of one's merits and demerits in all of his previous lives. ***Karma*** is debt that has to be paid over a lifetime or many lifetimes.

p. *16*
Kamsa, *King of Maduhra*, ***Krishna***'s uncle, slain by the nephew when his tyranny became unbearable

p.*18*
Narayana is one of ***Krishna***'s many names.

p.*19*
Devaki is ***Krishna***'s birthmother. ***Vasudeva*** is ***Krishna***'s birth father. On hearing that ***Kamsa***, ***Krishna***'s uncle and king of ***Madhura***, has ordered the slaughter of all new born babes in his kingdom, ***Vasudeva*** secretly transports infant ***Krishna*** to ***Nanda Gokula***, the scene of ***Krishna's*** childhood and many divine exploits.

p. *21*
The nine openings are the nine openings of the body. The six thieves are the deadly sins. The seven layered fortress
p. *25*
Dairy products, because the cow is holy, have a sacred significance for Hindus. **Janaka** *is the father of* **Sita**, *wife of* **Rama**, *who is an incarnation of* **Krishna**. **Kumkum** *is an ornamental powder worn on the forehead by Hindus.* **Venkataramana**, **Vishnu**, *resides at the top the range of seven hills in South India.*
Alagiri Ranga is Krishna.
p. *26*
Eight jewels worn in the ears, on the fingers, and arms; eight kin are father, mother, uncles, aunts, sisters, brothers, wife, nephews and nieces
p.*30*
Rukumangada is a staunch devotee of **Vishnu**. He sets himself a course of ascetic course of mediation on Vishnu. Brahma sends a most beautiful devine female, **Mohini** to distract him. **Rukumangada** offers to sacrifice his son rather than stray from his meditation.
The foe of **Baka** is **Bheema**, a founding deity of Purandaradasa's cult. The honorable monkey is **Hanuman**, another founding deity, **Rama**'s lieutenant who helped him build a bridge a link to Sri Lanka, where lived **Ravana** who kidnapped **Rama**'s wife, **Sita**.
Lakshmi is **Vishnu**'s spouse. **Bali** is known for his unlimited generosity. **Krishna**, disguised as a brahmin novice, asks him for enough land to take three steps. Turning into a gigantic figure, with the first step, he covers heaven, hell with the second, the third one he places on **Bali**'s head. **Prahlada** is the son of **Hiranyakashipu**, **Krishna**'s doorkeeper in a previous life and now his enemy. When **Hiranyakashipu** threatens to kill **Prahlada** for worshipping **Vishnu**, **Vishnu** appears in a half-lion, half-man form and slays **Hiranyakashipu**.
Arjuna is a nephew of **Krishna,** also the celebrated warrior who is the protagonist of the <u>Bhagavad Gita</u>.
p. *32*
Hari is one of Vishnu's innumerable appellations. *The Six Deadly Sins* are: Pride, lust, anger, envy, gluttony, and jealousy. **The three qualities** are best glossed as the processes of birth, growth, and death to which God is immune. *The eight manifestations of pride* are love of self, love of looks, love of money, love of property, love of position, love of knowledge, love of wife, love of children. **Keshava, Madhava** are among alternate epithets for **Krishna.**

p. 34
The dog is a metaphor for the human soul seeking salvation in the wrong things and in the wrong places.
p. 35
In moments of great distress, the speakers of many of the hymns resort to the explanation that the pain they experience in this life is a direct consequence of sins committed in previous lives, the number of each is determined for each individual by **Brahma**. **Brahma**'s fiat is believed to be invisibly inscribed on one's forehead.
p. 37
During each one of the legendary divisions of time, the existence of the universe is threatened by *asuras*, demons, the antithesis of *suras*, angels, and humans. Vishnu assumes the responsibility for saving the universe by appearing in different incarnations and slaying the the demons. **The Hill** is *Thirupathi*, a pilgrimage center in South India. Krishna is described as **Lotus-eyed** and **Lotus-footed** to emphasize his unsullied nature and beauty.
p. 41
The lord of lords, **Vishnu**, spends his time on earth as an ordinary cowherd, **Gopala.**
p. 42
A whole of herd of elephants is drinking water from a river. Their leader is being pulled into the river by a crocodile. **The King of Elephants** saves himself by reciting the name "*Adimula*," which means the beginning of all. *Draupadi*, the wife of **Krishna**'s five nephews, the **Pandavas**, is hauled before the **Kauravas**, the antagonists of the **Pandavas**, when the latter lose everything they have in a game of dice. The **Kauravas** try to strip Draupadi of her sari, threatening to rape her. When she throws her hands up and cries out "*Krishna*", thus expressing her faith in him, her sari turns into an endless garment. **Little Dhruva** is a child devotee banished to the forest by his father, who is a hater of **Krishna**.
p. 47
Yashoda is Krishna's foster mother.
p. 47
This is the lament of a sinful soul after departing from the world. **Home** is salvation; the **two wives** are worldly possessions; the **house** is the body; **the empty square** the little space occupied by it; **lumps of sugar** are worldly preoccupations.
p. 50
Gopalakrishna is the cowherd.

p. 51
Kama is the Hindu god of love, lust, desire
p. 54
Ranga is the popular south Indian version of the name ***Krishna.***
p. 55
Kauravas and Pandavas: two families of Krishna's nephews. The ***Kauravas*** symbolize evil and the ***Pandavas*** good. The families fought a fratricidal war. Krishna's protegees, the Pandavas won. ***Yama*** is the Hindu god of death.
p. 56
Vaikuntha is Vishnu's heavenly abode.
p.62
The ***boat*** is the human body with its nine holes; the ***river*** is life. The ***six waves*** are the six deadly sins. The ***five enemies*** are the five senses.
p. 63
The crowded city with its nine gates is the body; the five rulers are the five senses.
p. 64
The dog is the soul that has squandered its opportunity on earth.
p. 65.
Panchali is Draupadi; ***Ahalye*** turned into a rock by her husband who suspects her character. Krishna brings her back to life. Krishna is drives the **eagle-flagged** chariot for his nephew, Arjuna, in the war against the Kauravas. ***Ajamila*** is a sinful bramin who calls his son Narayana to aid him. Krishna, one of whose many names is Narayana, saves Ajamila from death.
p. 67
Tilaka is a short beauty mark placed on the forehead.

Dinesh Hassan is Associate Professor of English at Central State University, Wilberforce, Ohio, where he teaches literature, composition, and literary theory. Dinesh Hassan was born in Karnataka, India, in a household where Purandaradasa's songs and hymns informed almost every daily activity, from the most mundane to the most exalted, from dawn to dusk. This is the case with most Kannada speaking families in that part of that country. The strong presence of Purandaradasa provided the impetus here for transcreating this collection of hymns.

Hassan received his Ph.D. from the University of Cincinnati. His doctoral dissertation examines Shakespeare's early comedies from a deconstructionist angle, arguing they contain more concealed anxieties than festivity about Elizabethan England. He hopes to translate into English more Kannada religious poetry from different periods and different schools.

Other Titles in the Harmony Series
from Bottom Dog Press

When: Poems by Don Moyer
0-933087-81-0 96 pgs. $10.95

O Taste and See: Food Poems
edited by David Lee Garrison & Terry Hermsen
0-933087-82-9 198 pgs. $14.00

*Songs of the Woodcutter:
Zen Poems of Wang Wei and Taigu Ryokan*
by Larry Smith & Monte Page
0-933087-80-2 (CD & Booklet) $15.00

Song That Fathoms Home: Poems by Ray McNiece
0-933087-85-3 124 pgs. $12.00

Hymns of Purandaradasa
Translated by Dinesh Hassan
0-933087-89-6 88 pgs. $12.95

Bowl of Water: Poems by Allen Frost
0-933087-88-8 136 pgs. $12.95

Homepage for Ordering
http://members.aol.com/Lsmithdog/bottomdog
Include $1.50 with any order for shipping.

Supporting the Art of Writing